AF673309

SMART BRAIN RIGHT BRAIN

The Elements of Art

Om KIDZ
An imprint of Om Books International

Om Books International

Reprinted in 2023

Corporate & Editorial Office
A-12, Sector 64, Noida 201 301
Uttar Pradesh, India
Phone: +91 120 477 4100
Email: editorial@ombooks.com
Website: www.ombooksinternational.com

Sales Office
107, Ansari Road, Darya Ganj
New Delhi 110 002, India
Phone: +91 11 4000 9000
Email: sales@ombooks.com

Author: Swayam Ganguly
Editor: Nandita Bhardwaj
Art & Design: Anshuman Pandey, Gaurav Bhandari, Harish Arya

ISBN: 978-93-52768-50-9

Printed in India

10 9 8 7 6 5 4 3 2

CONTENTS

1. Elements of Art

Have you ever looked at a sculpture in an art gallery or a painting at the school exhibition and wondered how the artist created such a beautiful piece of art? Do you want to create one?

So, what is it that you require to create an artwork? What are these building blocks or tools? To create an artwork, you need the **Elements of Art**.

Seven Elements of Art

Line, Form, Colour, Shape, Texture, Space and Value are the seven basic elements of art.

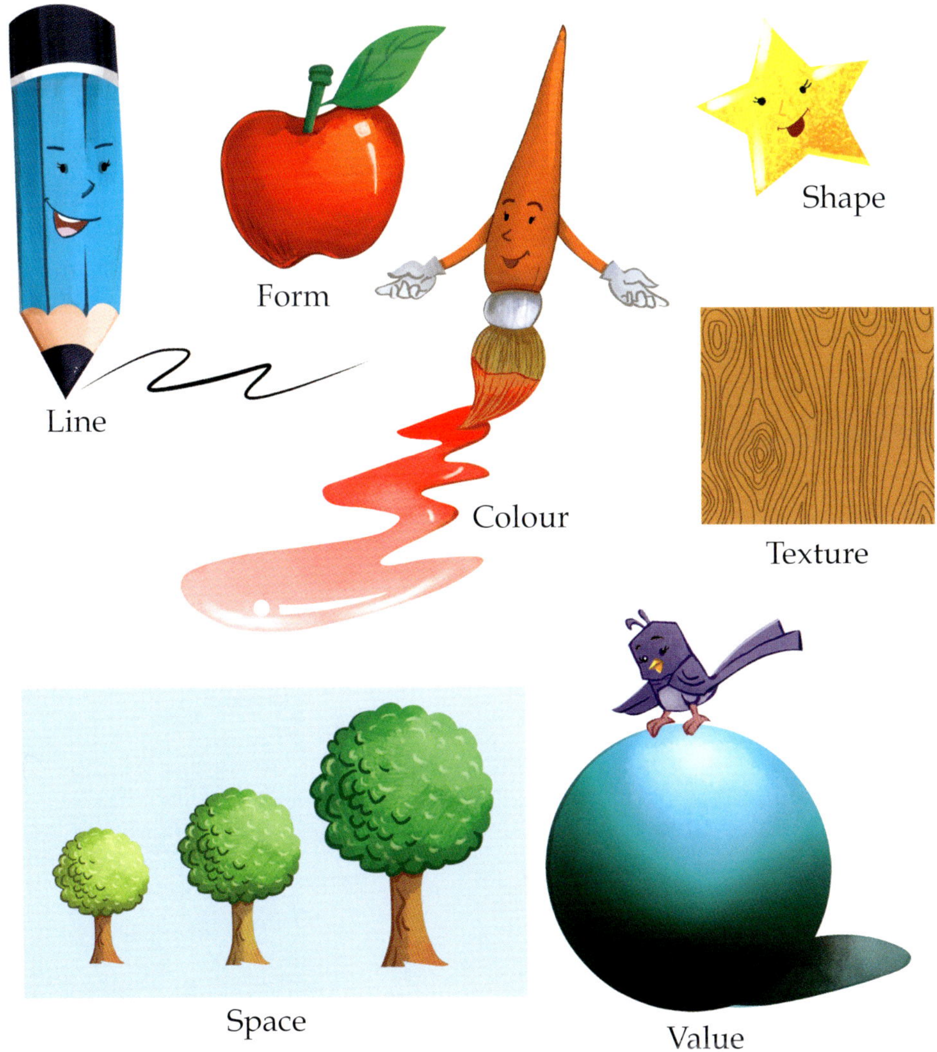

2. Why Does an Artist Use These Elements?

Every artist must use these seven elements to create art. But how does an artist use these elements? Just like a chef at a restaurant uses many ingredients to cook a special dish, an artist creates an artwork using these seven elements. Sometimes, an artist uses all the elements and sometimes only one or two elements are used.

A sculptor, unlike a painter, uses both form and space while creating a sculpture, because these elements are three-dimensional, and a must for sculpture; three-dimensional means to have length, width and depth.

A sculptor must use form and space, which are two of the seven elements of art to create a sculpture.

A painter can use some, but not all the elements of art to create a painting.

3. Why Are the Elements of Art Important?

The elements of art are important because we would not be able to create any sort of art without using at least a few of them. Secondly, learning what these elements are, helps us to:

- Describe the work of an artist.
- Understand why the artwork is special.
- Share our thoughts and ideas using a common language of art.

DID YOU KNOW?

Without these seven elements of art, there would be no art in our world.

4. Line

What is a line in art?
A line is a mark made by a drawing tool like a brush or a pencil.

Types of Lines

A line can be either straight or curved. But there are three other types of lines:

1. Descriptive Lines: These lines help us understand what we are seeing, for example, outlines, contour lines and single lines.

POCKET FACT

A line is a moving point.

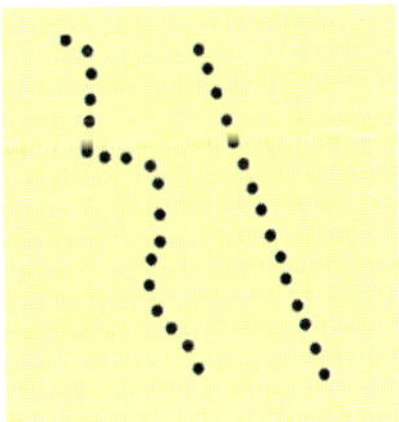

2. Implied Lines: These lines are not seen, but are indicated. A dotted line is an implied line.

3. Expressive Lines: These lines send us the artists' message as to how they want to make us feel through their art.

Lines add value

1. There are many types of lines, each varying in weight and character.

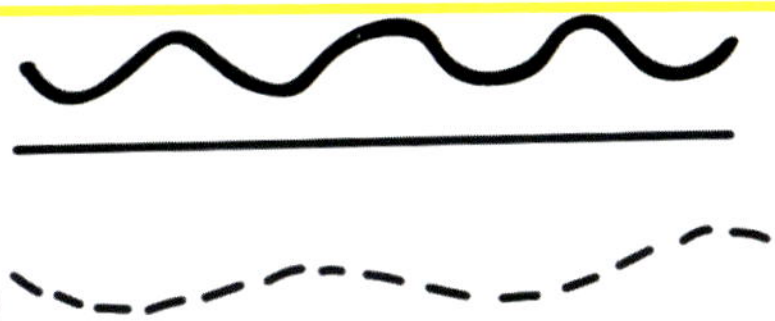

2. The points in an implied line are automatically connected by the eye.

3. When one object points to another, the eye connects the two in a psychic line.

Lines can be used to create two dimensions or three dimensions. Lines have an impact on the other elements of art, too.

When you use many types of lines in your artwork like continuous, broken, vertical, jagged, and horizontal lines, not only does your artwork become impressive, but it also makes an impact on the viewer's mind.

Learn to identify and use different lines

Use the worksheet below to practise seven examples of how lines can be used in different drawings. Can you think of more examples to add to this list? Happy line drawing!

1. Straight

2. Wavy

3. Dotted

4. Zigzag

5. Cloud

6. Castle

7. Curly Cues

Direction of line

The direction of a line can change an artwork dramatically. Diagonal lines create movement and energy. Horizontal and vertical lines add stability and strength to an artwork.

Diagonal lines create movement

Horizontal and vertical lines create stability

DID YOU KNOW?

We can use different types of lines to show when we are happy, sad or angry. That is, different lines can be used to show different emotions.

5. Shape

When you draw lines and close some of those lines, you create what is called a **shape**. The lines that you close make a shape, which is another element of art. For example, squares, triangles, circles and rectangles – are all shapes.

Shapes play an important role in creating art

Activity: To create a truck using different shapes

We can create many things by using different shapes like a triangle, circle, square or a rectangle. Let's see how we can create a truck using different shapes.

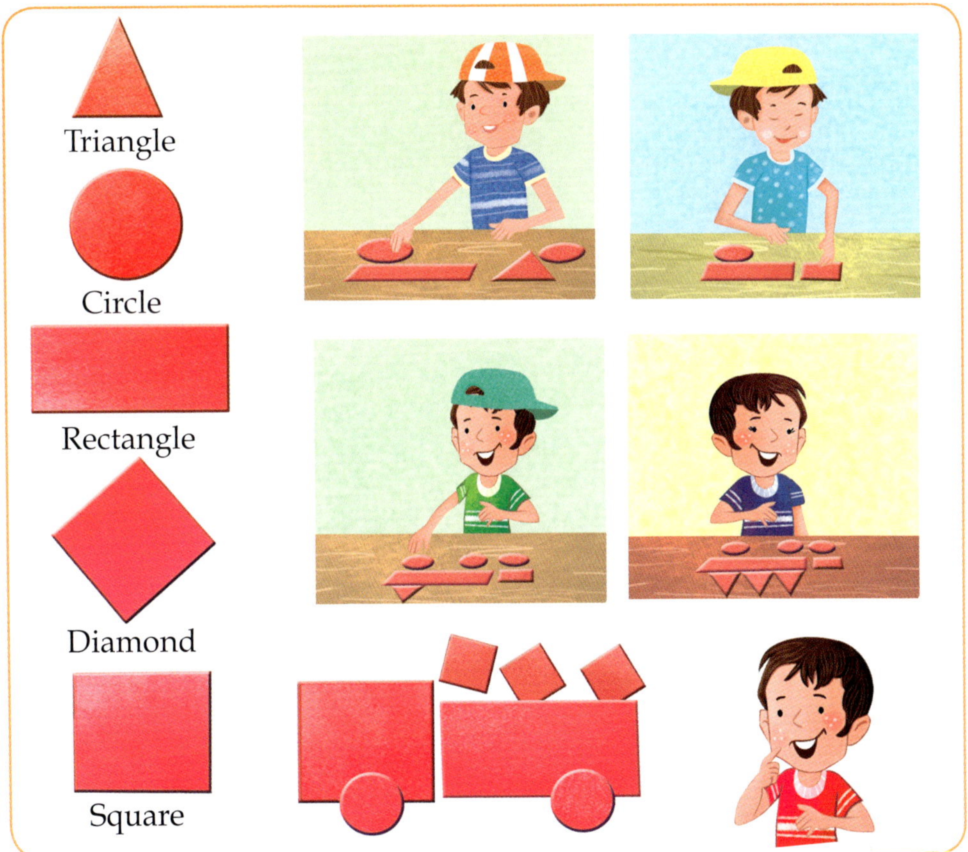

Shapes can be divided into two categories: **geometric** shapes and **organic** shapes.

POCKET FACT

Shapes are flat and they can only have length and width.

Geometric Shapes and Organic Shapes

Shapes may be either geometric or organic. The former are mathematical shapes like triangles, squares, and circles. The latter are those shapes that are not well-defined, or are those that are found in nature.

Geometric Shapes

Organic Shapes

What does a shape reveal?

Shapes reveal feelings in an artwork.

Squares and rectangles depict strength and stability. Squares and rectangles look strong and stable because these shapes are solid. They are also made up of straight lines and right angles that have a mathematical, balanced feel.

Straight lines and right angles make a shape look solid

Circles and ovals depict continuous movement as they have no beginning or end. They represent life and lifecycle. They are present in the form of the Sun, moon, Earth, and the other planets in our universe. They are also found in nature in the form of fruits and flowers.

Circles can move freely like wheels, balls and merry-go rounds. Circles have been used for generations to represent unity as in the Olympic Games logo.

Circles are also found in nature in fruits

Circles show movement

Triangles make the eye travel upwards

Triangles depict an upward movement and show both power and energy like in arrows, as well as in the great Egyptian Pyramids.

6. Space

While drawing, if you think you should vary the size of your lines and shapes or where you are placing them in your drawing, you must use another element of art which is known as **space** and is not to be confused with outer space.

In your artwork, you might overlap some shapes to make them appear closer than they are, or make distant objects smaller to give the impression that they are far away.

Positive Space and Negative Space

The space within the object is called positive space. The area around an object is called negative space.

Positive Space

Negative Space

POCKET FACT

The subject of a work of art is the positive space. The space which is not used in an artwork is the negative space.

7. Value

So far you have used three elements of art to create your artwork, that is, line, shape and space. But you are not totally satisfied with your work. You think about using your pencil and darkening some lines or shading a part of your artwork. Then, you use your eraser to lighten some areas. There! You have just used the fourth element of art called **value**.

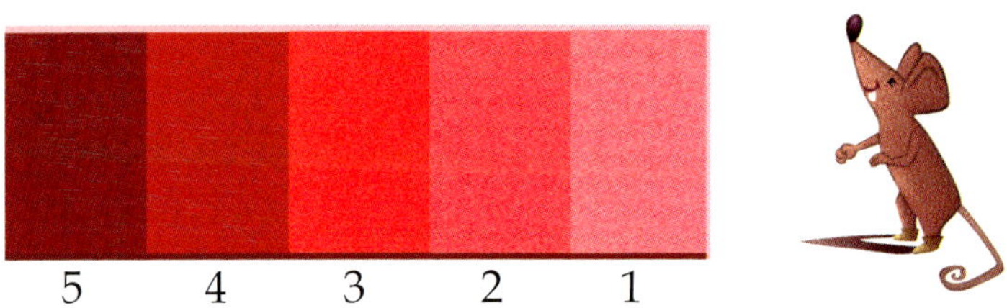

Many artists use a value scale to create the full range of value.

Value deals with light and we can see things because light reflects off things. Without light we cannot see anything. Value creates the illusion of light in a painting. Value is also essential to drawing and painting for it creates contrast, which helps in producing a point of interest in an artwork.

What is value?

Value is the use of light and dark in an artwork. Value is also known as '**tone**'.

The use of value is extremely important in art; it helps you see objects and creates an impact in your artwork.

POCKET FACT

White is the lightest value and black is the darkest value. The difference between them is known as contrast.

8. Form

What if you decide that instead of drawing something, you will create a sculpture instead? The basic difference between a flat drawing and a sculpture is that a sculpture can be seen from many viewpoints. A sculpture can be viewed from the front, back, and the sides. When you are creating a sculpture, you use the element of **form**.

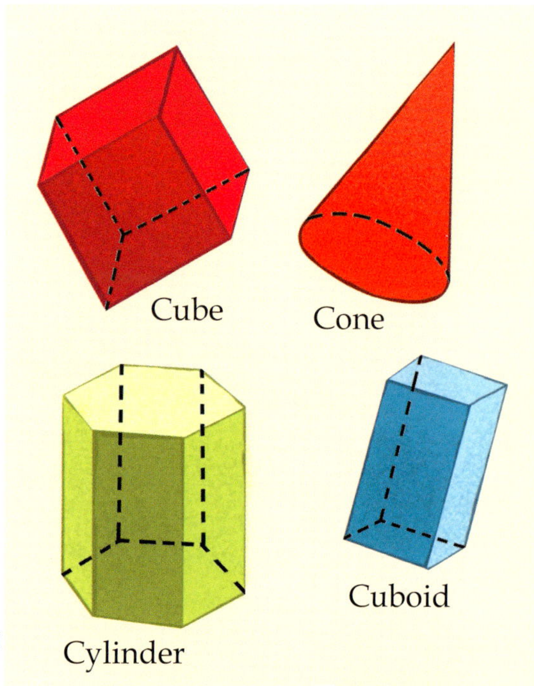

POCKET FACT

Form has not only length and width, but also depth.

What is Form?

The three-dimensional version of a shape is called form. Suppose you fill air in a square, and make it a cube, it would be called a form.

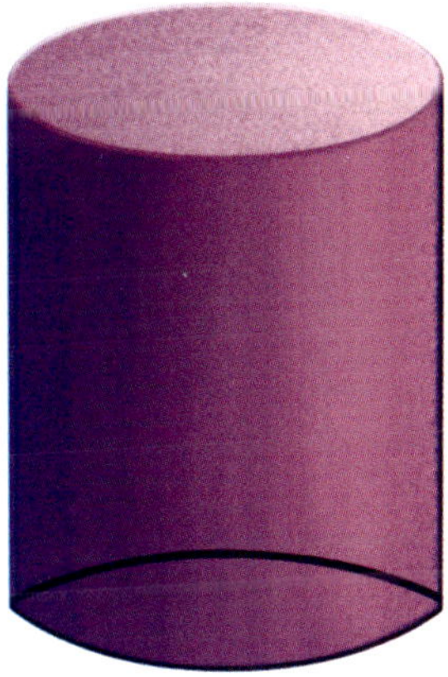

Cylinder

Cone

An artwork that is not flat and can be seen from different angles has the art element of form. Forms can have hard edges like a cube or can be free flowing. Cylinders, pyramids and spheres are some of the common forms and are called geometric forms. Organic forms are shapes that may look like leaves, flowers, clouds—things that grow, flow, and move.

Leaf

Flower

Cloud

Organic Forms

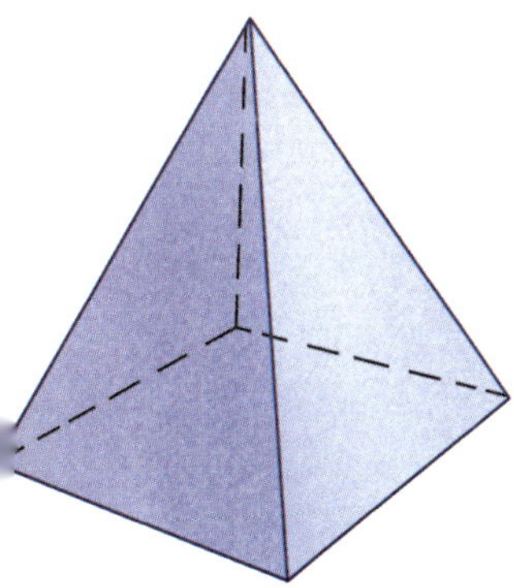

Pyramids are geometric forms.

POCKET FACT

Form generally refers to sculpture, 3D design and architecture but can also be the illusion of 3D on a 2D surface.

9. Colour

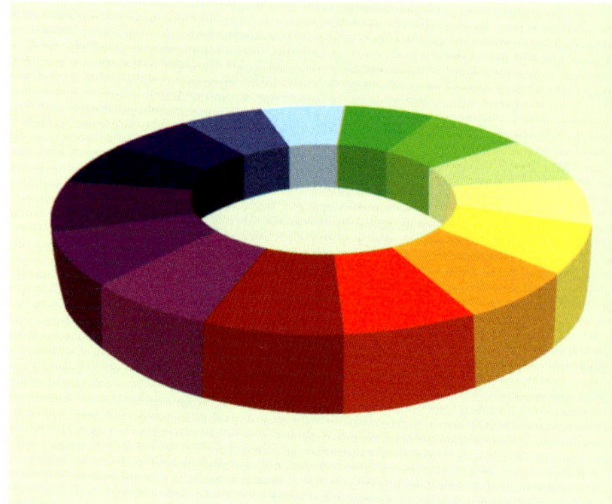

Colour is the visual element that has the strongest effect on our artwork and emotions. We use colour to create the mood or atmosphere in an artwork.

Blue is a cool colour

Yellow and orange are warm colours

Colour is thought to be the most important element because it makes the viewers feel a certain way about the artwork or painting that they see. For example, a painting can be cold or warm, or it can display other emotions.

The three building blocks of colours are **hue**, **value** and **intensit** and you can create many emotions and feelings using these. In art, colour can be used either as a symbol, or to create a pattern. It can create a mood or set up contrast in a painting.

POCKET FACT

Colour is the element of art that is produced when light, striking an object, is reflected to the eye.

Hue is the colour itself (blue, red, green).

Value is the hue's lightness or darkness and changes when white or black is added to it (range of light and dark).

Intensity is the hue's brightness or darkness (range of bright and dark).

Colour Theory

The Colour Theory was first suggested in the 17th century by the great mathematician and scientist Sir Issac Newton, who discovered that white light could be divided into a spectrum by passing it through a prism.

The study of colour in art and design often starts with the colour theory. Colour theory splits up colours into three categories: primary, secondary, and tertiary.

DID YOU KNOW?

All the colours are present in white light. We understand colours from the light reflected off objects. A red object, for example, looks red because it reflects the red part of the light. It would be a different colour under a different light.

10. Texture

Texture is the surface quality of an artwork. It is the roughness or smoothness of the material from which it is made. Texture shows how your art object, or element, in a composition would feel or look when touched or viewed.

Some examples of texture can be described as furry, bumpy, brittle, smooth, rough, soft, and hard.

Bumpy

Brittle

Smooth

Furry

There are many forms of texture. But the two main forms are **Actual texture** and **Visual texture**. Texture can be natural or artificial (human-made).

Texture is the way something feels to the touch or looks to the eye

POCKET FACT

It is difficult to recreate the shiny surface of glass or metal or the rough feel of a rock. Using the other elements of art, namely, line, colour and tone help a painter to define the texture.

Visual and Actual Texture

Visual texture is two-dimensional, and can be seen but not felt. Actual texture, or tactile texture, is texture that can not only be seen, but can also be felt.

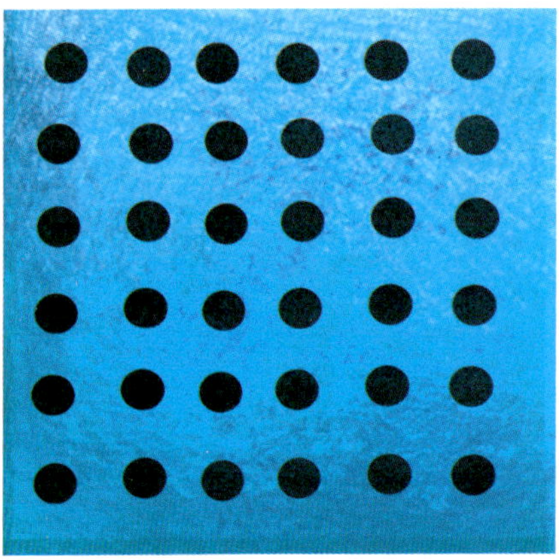

Texture is important in painting to make objects appear real

POCKET FACT

Texture can be experienced in two ways: optically (through sight) and physically (through touch).

Relationship between the Visual Elements

All the elements are related to each other in the following way:

- Most images begin as line drawings.
- Lines crossover one another to form shapes.
- Shapes can be filled with tone and colour, or repeated to create patterns.
- A shape may be rendered with a rough surface to create a texture.
- A shape may be projected into three dimensions to create form.

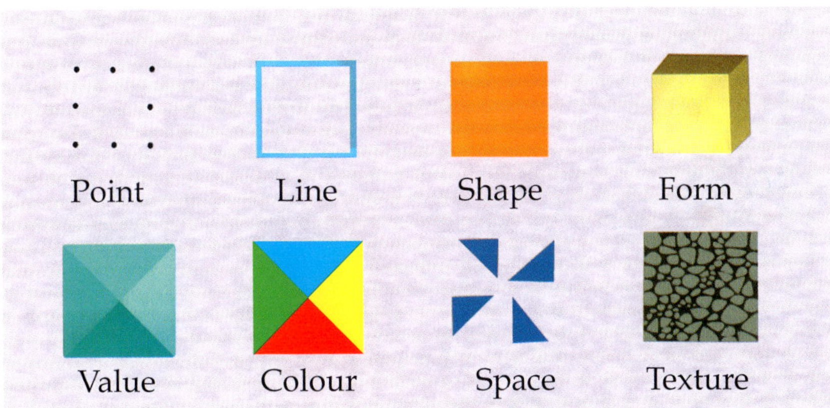

DID YOU KNOW?

Some artists create art that is displayed in museums or galleries. Other artists produce art for books, movies, commercials and websites. Even products like your breakfast cereal are packaged in boxes that are designed by artists.

11. Practise and Learn

- Study the works of great artists like Picasso, Michelangelo, Leonardo da Vinci, Renoir and Monet.
- Draw straight lines, curvy lines and angled lines on different index cards with a marker. Then glue the cards on a big piece of coloured paper. This will help you remember the different kinds of lines you can use in your artwork.
- Play with clay dough and make shapes with it which will teach you more about form.
- When you study any artwork, try and look for a variety of shapes and forms.
- Learn more about colour by looking at the art that uses the warm colour family (oranges, reds and yellows) and then the cool colour family (blues, greens and purples). Study the works of painters like van Gogh who used colour to change the mood of art.

- To explore more about texture, use a sponge, brush or finger paints.

Quiz

Elements of Art

1. What are primary colours?

2. What are the secondary colours?

3. Draw three geometric shapes.

4. Draw two organic shapes.

5. Draw a blue horizontal line.

6. Draw a green vertical line.

7. Draw a red diagonal line.

8. Draw a quick sketch that shows depth or space.

Match the definition with the correct element:

1.	An element that refers to the way things feel, or look, as they might feel, if touched	Geometric shapes
2.	An element of art that refers to a line that connects back to itself	Cool colours
3.	Reminds us of ice or grass (blue, green, violet)	Value
4.	An element that refers to the distance between, around, above, below and within things	Space
5.	An element that reminds us of the sun and warmth (red, yellow, orange)	Shape
6.	The path of moving point through space	Warm colours
7.	Shapes that were made with a ruler or are very precise and have a name	Texture
8.	The lightness or darkness of a hue	Organic shapes
9.	Shapes that are not regular or even, they are free-form	Form
10.	An element that refers to an object with three dimensions	Line

Turn the following shapes into forms by adding colour and value. Also identify the final forms.

Shape **Form** **Name**

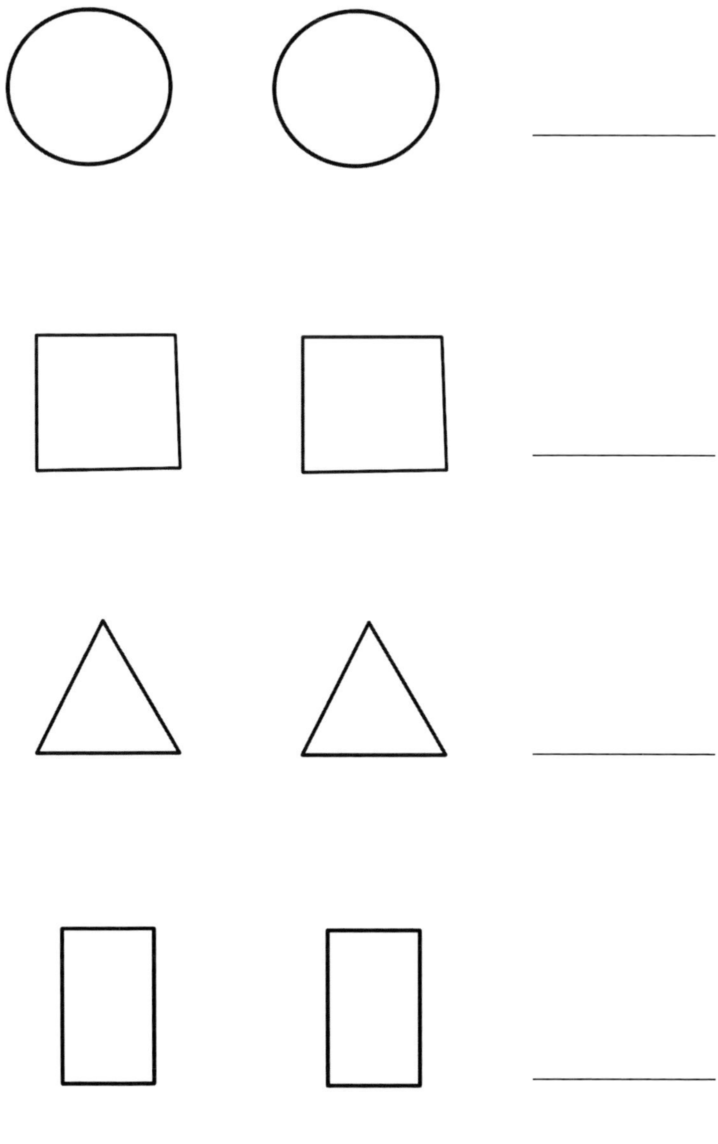

GLOSSARY

Implied	suggested
Expressive	conveying a special quality or idea
Dimension	a measurement such as length, width or depth
Organic	consisting of or relating to living plants and animals, or the substances of which they are made
Spectrum	band of colours as seen in a rainbow
Prism	a transparent glass that separates white light that passes through it into different colours
Sculpture	the art of making two- or three-dimensional forms, especially by carving stone or wood or by casting metal or plaster

ANSWERS

Page 29. 1. Red, Blue, Yellow.

2. Purple, Orange, Green

3. 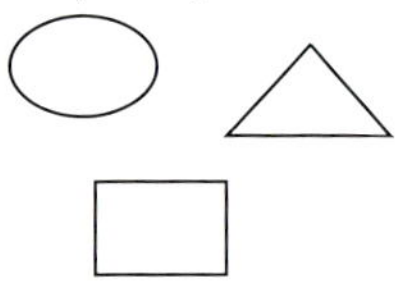

4. Shapes

5.

6.

7. 

8. 

Page 30.
1. Texture
2. Shape
3. Cool colours
4. Space
5. Warm colours
6. Line
7. Geometric shapes
8. Value
9. Organic shapes
10. Form

Page 31.

	Name	Form
	1. Sphere	
	2. Cubc	
	3. Cone	
	4. Cylinder	